Making Rhythm Easy

by Victoria McArthur
with Edwin McLean

learn to play, write,
and hear rhythm
through motivating activities

Contents

RHYTHM PLACEMENT EVALUATION

*This **optional** pretest is for students with prior music experience.*

To the teacher:

Before beginning this book, you may wish to give your student this pretest.
The test answers can be written or verbalized by the student.
Examples missed will target where you may wish to begin this book with each student.
(Pages are indicated in the right-hand margin.)

Start at page:

1. Tap 8 steady beats at an *andante* tempo.   5

2. Tap and count this rhythm aloud: 6

3. What is 𝅗𝅥 called, and how many beats does it get in $\frac{4}{4}$ time?   7

_____ note   _____ beat(s)

4. What is 𝄾 called, and how many beats does it get in $\frac{4}{4}$ time?   11

_____ rest   _____ beat(s)

5. What does the time signature $\frac{3}{4}$ mean?   13

3 means _____   4 means _____

6. Where is the strong beat in $\frac{2}{4}$ time?   13

_____

7. What is this symbol ⌢ called, and what does it mean?   17

name _____ meaning _____

Start at page:

8. What is 𝅘𝅥𝅭. called, and how many beats does it get in $\frac{4}{4}$ time?   18

_____ _____ note _____ beat(s)

9. Tap and count this rhythm aloud: 18

$\frac{4}{4}$ 𝅘𝅥𝅭. 𝅘𝅥𝅮 𝅘𝅥𝅭. 𝅘𝅥𝅮 | 𝅘𝅥 𝅘𝅥 𝅘𝅥 𝅘𝅥 𝅘𝅥𝅭. 𝄾 ‖

10. What is 𝄽· called, and how many beats does it get in $\frac{4}{4}$ time?   21

_____ _____ rest _____ beat(s)

11. What does $\frac{2}{2}$ mean?   25

The top 2 means _____. The bottom 2 means _____.

12. Draw another symbol for $\frac{4}{4}$ time.   _____   25

13. What does *accel.* mean? _____   33

14. What does *rit.* mean? _____   33

UNIT 1

PULSE

Music has a steady pulse like your heartbeat.

TAKING THE PULSE

Ask your teacher to turn the metronome on to 80.

Tap (with both hands in your lap) 8 steady beats with energy as you hear and feel the steady click.

Beats are like the steady pulse in music.

PULSE AND RHYTHM

1. Tap 8 steady beats with your left hand only.

2. Tap this rhythm with your right hand only.

3. Now tap lines 1 and 2, hands together.
   Hint: Read line 2 as you tap the steady ♩ pulse with your left hand.

TEMPO

Ask your teacher to turn the metronome to 40.
- Tap 8 steady beats with energy. Listen for the slow, steady pulse.

- Now tap 8 steady beats with the metronome set at 100.

- Finally, tap 8 steady beats with the metronome set at 180.
  Keep the pulse steady!

You just tapped 8 steady beats three different ways.
How was each different?
(Each example had the pulse beating at a different speed.)

Tempo is the word musicians use to describe the speed of the pulse in music.
Musicians often use Italian words for different speeds (*tempi*).

Three examples are:

     Largo (LAHR-goh)   Slow   ♩ = 40–60

     Andante (ahn-DAHN-tay)   Walking speed   ♩ = 76–108

   *Presto* (PREH-stoh)   Very fast   ♩ = 144–200

6

Tap Dancers in Review

Tap using both hands on both legs.
Listen to the steady pulse of the metronome (♩ = 80).

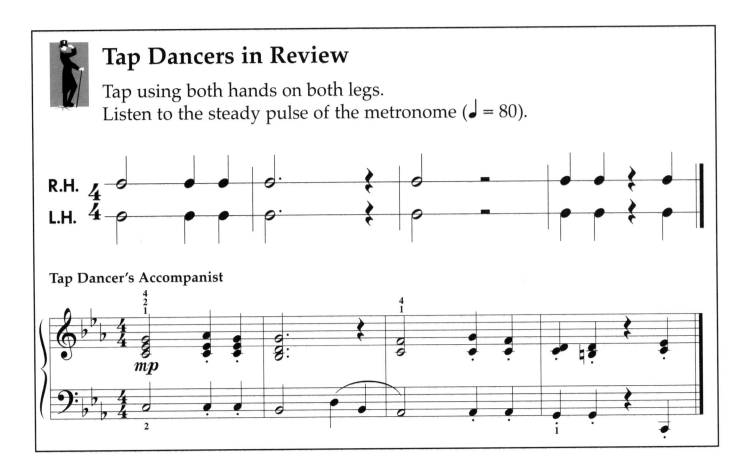

More Tap Dancers

Tap a steady beat (♩ = 60) with your *left* hand as your *right* hand taps the rhythm. Circle the correct tempo term: *largo*

andante

presto

Reverse hands and tap a steady beat (♩ = 100) with your *right* hand as your *left* hand taps the rhythm. (You may wish to turn the book upside down for extra fun.) Circle the correct tempo term: *largo*

andante

presto

THE EIGHTH NOTE

Sometimes music needs shorter note values than quarter notes.
Notice that an eighth note looks like a quarter note,
except it has a flag on its stem.

Eighth Notes

 flag   flag

Two or more
eighth notes
use a beam.

      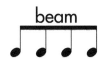

DISCOVERING THE SOUND

Tap the rhythm below with the metronome (♩ = 120).
(Remember that half notes last two beats.)
Tap with both hands.

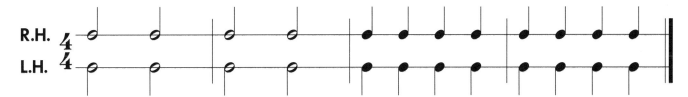

Now tap the rhythm below using quarter and eighth notes. (♩ = 120)
Say the words *walk* and *trotting*.
Hint: The rhythm below will sound and feel like the one you just tapped,
only faster.

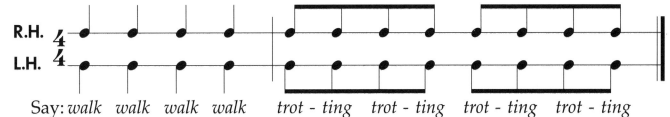

Say: *walk   walk   walk   walk   trot - ting   trot - ting   trot - ting   trot - ting*

8

THE EIGHTH WONDER OF THE WORLD

Imitate the tapping and speaking that your teacher does.

Teacher's Example (to be tapped and spoken aloud with metronome) ♩ = 100

Say: *"walk   walk   trot-ting   trot-ting   walk   walk   trot-ting   trot-ting"*

Repeat the example above at a faster tempo. (♩ = 144)

To the Student:
Did you notice that the tempo was faster the second time you tapped the example? You still tapped the same rhythm, however.

COUNTING ON EIGHTH NOTES!

In the examples above you said words for quarter and eighth notes.
You can also use numbers or syllables.

Review		Count	or	Say
Whole note	𝅝	*"one-two-three-four"*		*"tah-ah-ah-ah"*
Dotted half note	𝅗𝅥. or	*"one-two-three"*		*"tah-ah-ah"*
Half note	𝅗𝅥 or	*"one-two"*		*"tah-ah"*
Quarter note	𝅘𝅥 or	*"one"*		*"tah"*

New

Eighth notes	𝅘𝅥𝅮𝅘𝅥𝅮 or	*"one-and"*		*"tah-tay"*
	𝅘𝅥𝅮 or	*"one"* or *"and"*		*"tah"* or *"tay"*

(Notice that one eighth note gets the count of *one* **or** *and*.)

RHYTHM WIZARD

Fill in the blanks.
Hint: The wizard's hat contains the answers!

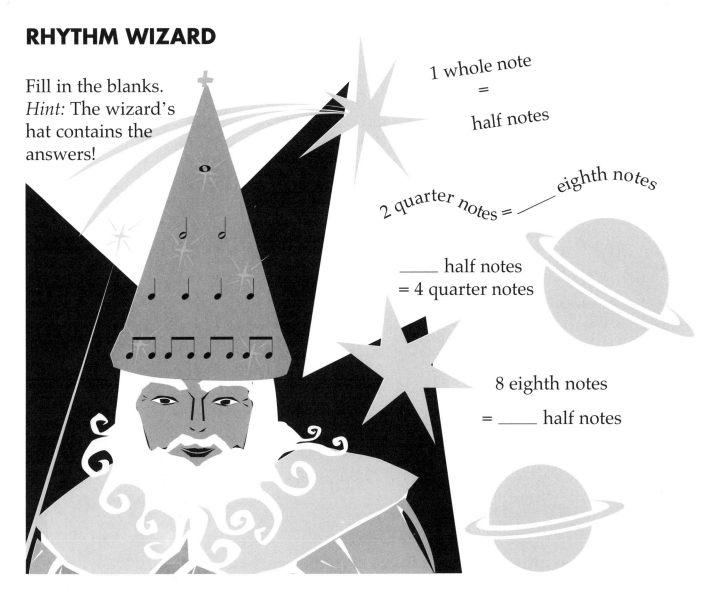

1 whole note
=
_____ half notes

2 quarter notes = _____ eighth notes

_____ half notes = 4 quarter notes

8 eighth notes = _____ half notes

COUNTING ON EIGHTH NOTES

Tap and count the rhythm below.
Count *1 and 2 and 3 and,* and so on.

R.H. $\frac{4}{4}$

Count: *1 and 2 and 3 and 4 and   1 and 2 and 3 and 4 and   1 and 2 and 3 and 4 and*

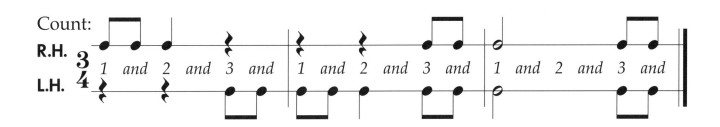

Count:
R.H. $\frac{3}{4}$
L.H.

1 and 2 and 3 and   1 and 2 and 3 and   1 and 2 and 3 and

MUSIC MATH

Add up the beats:

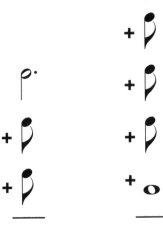

Answer:

2			

TROUBLE SHOOTER

Decide if your teacher taps the correct rhythm.
Circle **RIGHT or WRONG**.

Teacher: Tap incorrectly in at least one example. Set the metronome
at ♩ = 80 and count aloud 2 measures before tapping.

1.  **RIGHT   WRONG**
(circle one)

2. **RIGHT   WRONG**
(circle one)

3.  **RIGHT   WRONG**
(circle one)

THE EIGHTH REST 𝄾

Remember that music has periods of silence called **rests**.
Every note in music has an equal rest that is its partner.

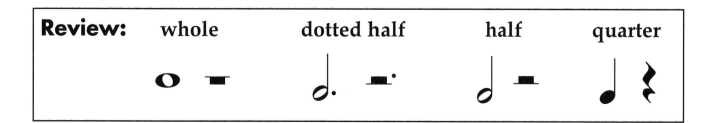

Review: whole   dotted half   half   quarter

You will not tap for rests, but you will still feel the steady pulse.
Remember to say *sh* for each beat of rest.

Write the counts under each rest.

Counts: *1   2   3-4*
Say: *sh   sh   sh-sh*

The **eighth rest** looks like this 𝄾   ♪ = ½ beat
It lasts as long as the eighth note, ½ beat.   𝄾 = ½ beat

Eine Kleine Rest

Write the counts.
Then tap and count aloud.

Counts: 1 and 2 and 3 and

Complete the melody below by writing in the missing rests.
Then tap and count.

Eine Kleine Nachtmusik (A Little Night Music)

Every satellite on the space station must equal **two beats**!

Draw flags, beams, stems, or darken noteheads so that each equals two beats only.

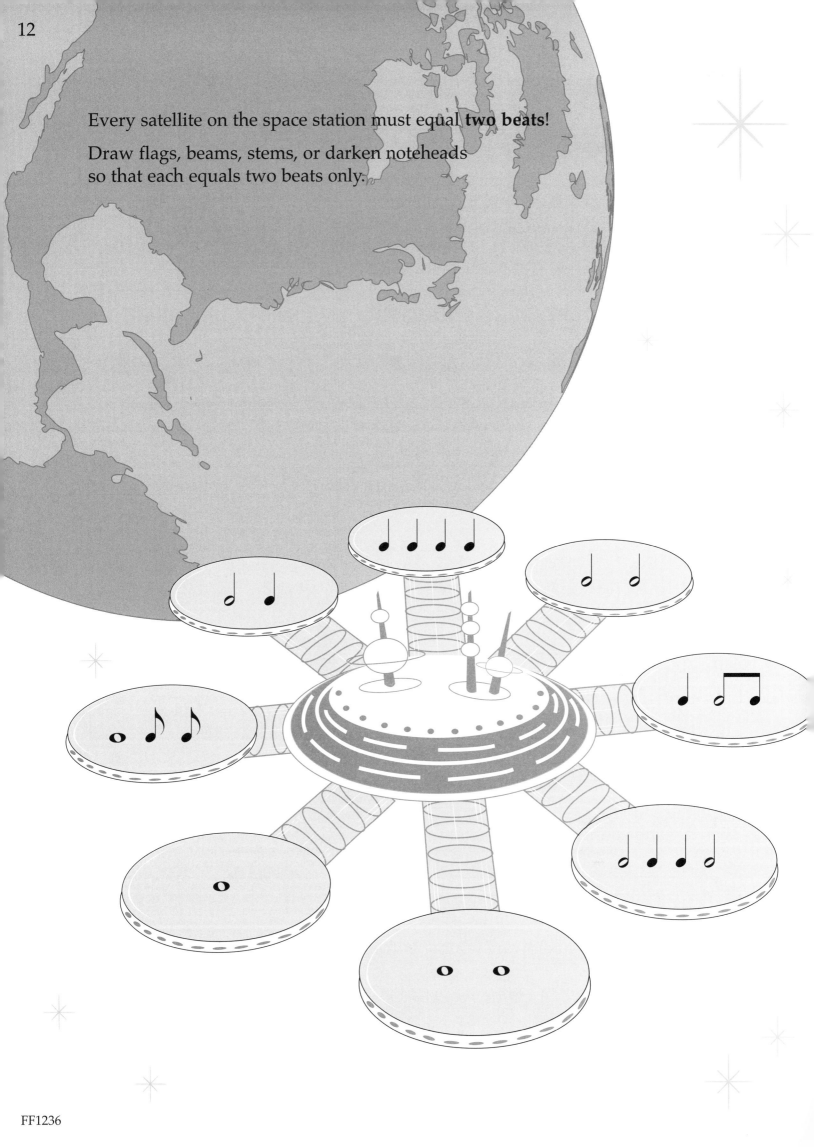

$\frac{2}{4}$ TIME*

Remember that the time (or meter) signature tells
the number of beats in each measure.
For each measure, the first beat is stronger than the others.

READING THE METER

Remember that $\frac{4}{4}$ means that the strong beats are four beats apart.
The bottom number, 4, means the quarter note gets one beat.

Remember that $\frac{3}{4}$ means that the strong beats are three beats apart.
The bottom number, 4, means the quarter note gets one beat.

"COUNT ME IN TWO!"

Tap the rhythm below.

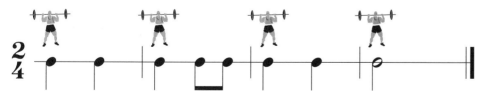

You just tapped a rhythm with the strong beats two beats apart.
This is called $\frac{2}{4}$ **time** or $\frac{2}{4}$ **meter**.

*Teacher:
  Conventional time signatures such as $\frac{2}{4}$, $\frac{3}{4}$, $\frac{4}{4}$ are used throughout this book.
  Book 1 used the alternate form ($\frac{3}{2}$, $\frac{4}{2}$ etc.) as an introduction to basic time signatures.

TIME TRAVELER

Solve each musical challenge as you travel through time.

Ancient Times (5000 years ago)
Great Sphinx

Write the time signature in the camel.

Early Times (2000 years ago)
Rome

Find the hidden rests and add up their beats.

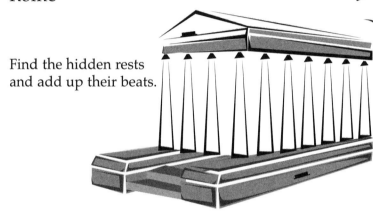

Middle Times (800 years ago)
Robin Hood and his Merry Men

 = _____ beats

Time of Columbus
Discovery of America (1492)

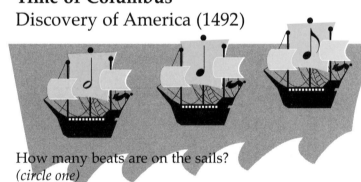

How many beats are on the sails?
(circle one)

4   3½   2½   5

Old Times
The Gold Rush of 1848

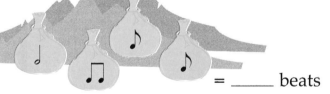 = _____ beats

Add up the bags of gold.

Modern Times
Trip to the Moon (1969)

Put missing notes and rests in the spaceship.

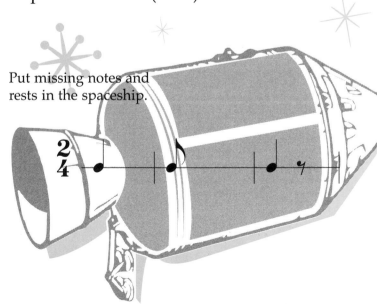

Present Times

Circle the correct time signature below.

$\frac{2}{4}$ $\frac{3}{4}$ $\frac{4}{4}$

_____
write today's date

ERROR BLASTER

Put an X through each incorrect rhythm.
Then write the rhythm correctly below. Tap and count it for extra credit!

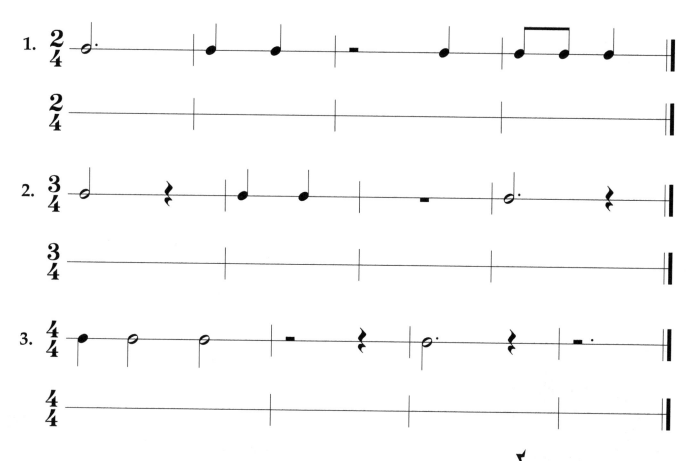

RHYTHMIC EARS

Circle the example that your teacher taps.

Teacher: Count 2 measures aloud before tapping.

Tap Dancers

Tap the rhythm below with your left hand as you count aloud.
Notice the dynamic marks.

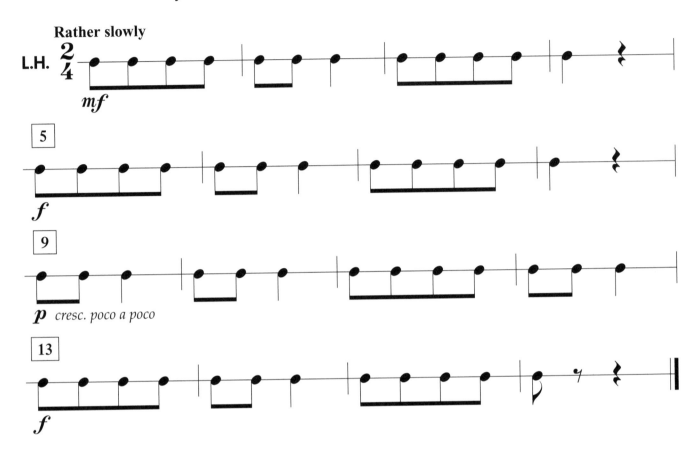

Tap Dancer's Accompanist

Old MacDonald

THE TIE

Remember that a tie connects two notes that have the same pitch.
Tap or play the first note, then hold it through the tied beats.

3 beats   **4 beats**

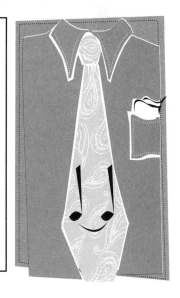

TIED UP!

Tap and count the rhythms below.
Watch out for ties!

THE TIE PUZZLER

Write the number of beats.

𝅝 — 𝅘𝅥 = ____ beats   𝅗𝅥. — 𝅘𝅥𝅮 𝅘𝅥 = ____ beats

𝅘𝅥𝅮 — 𝅘𝅥𝅮 𝅘𝅥 = ____ beats   𝅗𝅥 — 𝅗𝅥. — 𝅘𝅥𝅮 = ____ beats

UNIT 7

Discovering the Sound

Tap the rhythms below.

R.H.

L.H.

R.H.

L.H.

R.H.

L.H.

THE DOTTED QUARTER NOTE

Sometimes musicians want to write one note to equal 3 tied eighth notes.
This note is called a **dotted quarter note**.

It looks like this:

1 and 2   1 and 2

The dot adds one half of the note onto itself.

1½ beats   1   +   ½

Tap and count:

1 and 2 and 3 and 4 and

Tap Dancers

Tap the rhythm with your right hand as you count aloud.

1 and 2 and 3 and 4 and etc.

Tap Dancer's Accompanist

Theme from the New World Symphony — Dvořák

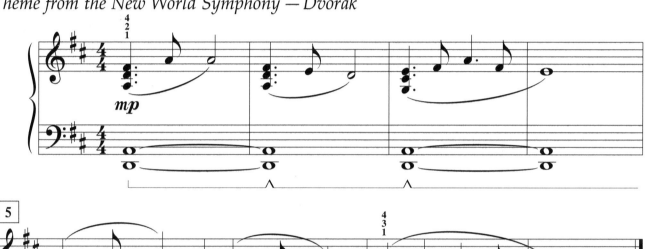

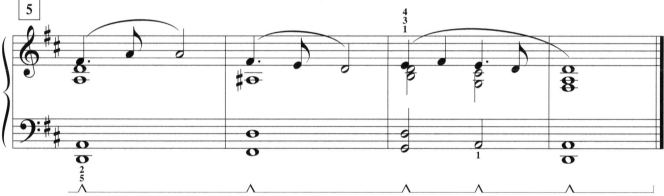

MUSIC MATH

Add the beats below.

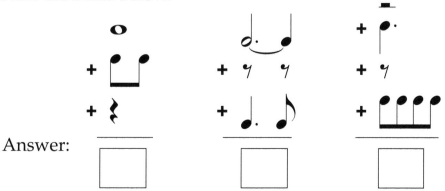

Answer:

PHONE TAPS

Tap and count, hands separately.

R.H.

L.H.

RHYTHM STORY

The Summer Cookout

Recipe for Grilled Hamburgers
(Add the notes and rests.)

✔ Ingredients needed: _____ pounds of lean hamburger

_____ fresh buns

✔ Prepare the meat ahead of time with:

_____ cup of soy or Worcestershire sauce

_____ teaspoon each of seasoned salt and pepper

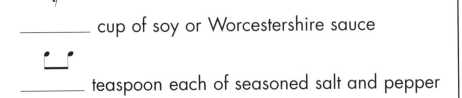

✔ Grill over medium coals for approximately _____ minutes.

Enjoy!

Answers: 2 pounds hamburger, 8 buns, 1/2 cup soy sauce, 1 teaspoon salt and pepper, 13 minutes

THE DOTTED QUARTER REST

The dotted quarter rest looks like this:

It lasts as long as the dotted quarter note—1 and ½ beats.

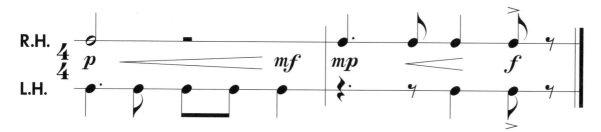

FOR COUNTING OUT LOUD!

Tap and count aloud the example below, hands together.
Notice the dynamics!

R.H.

L.H.

MORE ABOUT TEMPO

You have learned three tempo terms:

> *largo* means slow
>
> *andante* means walking speed
>
> *presto* means very fast

Here are three other common terms:

> *lento* - slow, faster than *largo* - ($\downarrow$ = 52–76)
>
> *moderato* - moderately, faster than *andante* - ($\downarrow$ = 84–120)
>
> *allegro* - lively, quick - ($\downarrow$ = 120–144)

GIVE YOUR EARS A REST

Circle the example that your teacher plays or taps.

Tap Dancers Need a Rest Too!

Tap and count the rhythm below, hands together.

Tap Dancer's Accompanist

Theme from Piano Concerto No. 1 — Tchaikovsky

23

MIX 'n' MATCH

Match each term on the left with its symbol on the right
by drawing a connecting line.

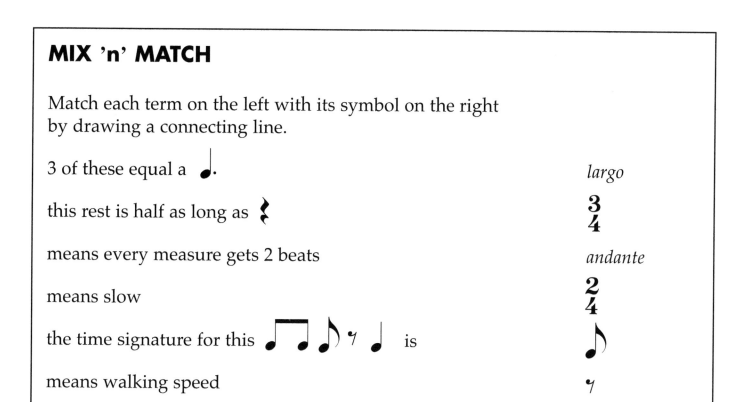

COUNT ME IN!

Write the counts (beats) for the music below.
Then tap (or play) and count aloud.
For extra credit, write the song titles.

A RHYTHM TREASURE HUNT

Match the music with the time signature by
drawing a connecting line to the correct treasure chest.

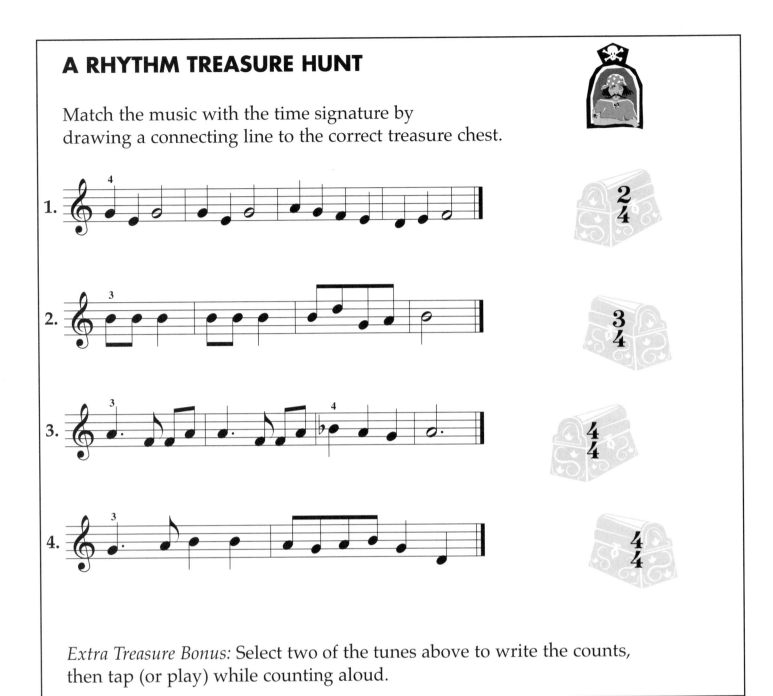

Extra Treasure Bonus: Select two of the tunes above to write the counts,
then tap (or play) while counting aloud.

NAME THAT TUNE!

Guess the name of the tune by tapping and counting the rhythm.

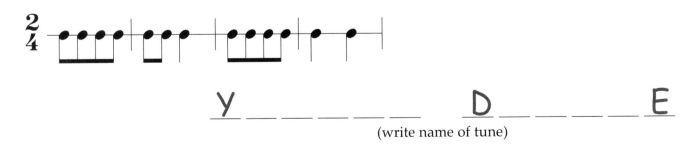

Y _ _ _ _ _   D _ _ _ _ E

(write name of tune)

$\frac{2}{2}$ TIME

Sometimes musicians want two beats in a measure, just as in $\frac{2}{4}$, but they want the *half* note to get one beat instead of the *quarter* note. This is especially useful in fast music.

This time signature is called $\frac{2}{2}$ **time**.

The symbol $\mathbb{C}$ means **cut time**.

It is another name for $\frac{2}{2}$.

Fill in the blanks below:

The top 2 means _____ beats in each measure.

The bottom 2 means the _____ gets one beat.
        (draw)

There is another symbol often used in place of $\frac{4}{4}$ time.

It looks like $\mathbb{C}$ and is called **common time**.

DISCOVERING THE SOUND

Presto (Note: Teacher and/or student taps example.)

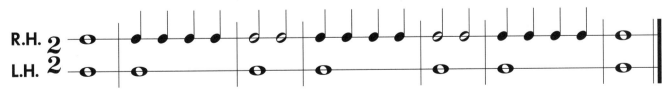

Did you notice that the tempo was fast in the music above?
Music written in $\frac{2}{2}$ is often fast, since the half note gets one beat.

FF1236

26

Tap Dancers

Tap and count:

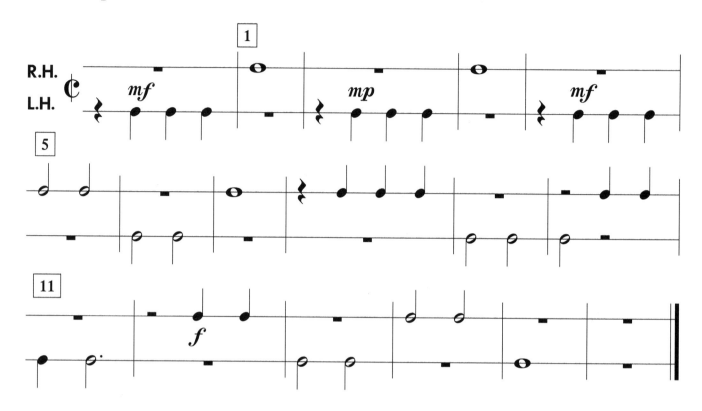

Tap Dancer's Accompanist

When the Saints Go Marching In

THE "WRITE" TIME

Draw bar lines in the examples below.

SHARP EARS

Your teacher will play a rhythm for you.
Circle either **a** or **b**.

BEETHOVEN IS COUNTING ON YOU!

Ludwig van Beethoven needs help finishing some of his music!
Help him by answering each question.

1. The symbol ₵ means _____ time. (Write the symbol in the music below.)
2. The Italian word for fast is _____. (Write the tempo marking in the music.)
3. Draw bar lines in the music.

After writing, play (or tap) the music below, counting aloud.

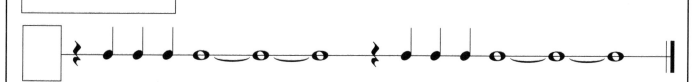

Extra Credit: Circle the name of this famous music: *Furry Leaves*
Fifth Symphony
Ode to Joey

Answer: Fifth Symphony

WORDS OF RHYTHM

Say the words below as you tap the rhythm.

Hint: Tap two measures of steady pulse before tapping the rhythm.

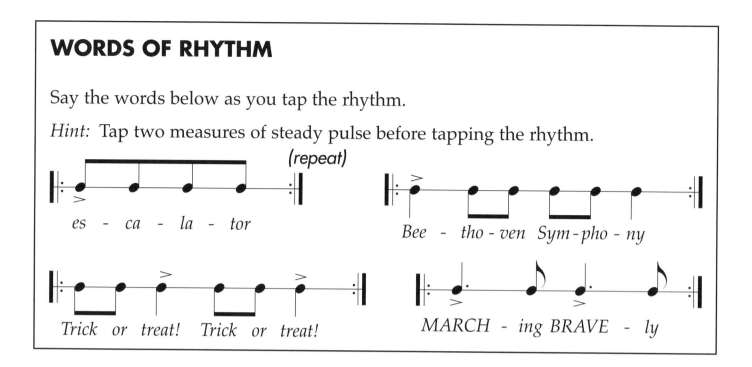

es - ca - la - tor

Bee - tho - ven Sym - pho - ny

Trick or treat! Trick or treat!

MARCH - ing BRAVE - ly

RHYTHM SAYINGS

Say the words below as you tap the rhythm.

Hint: Tap two measures of steady pulse before tapping the rhythm.

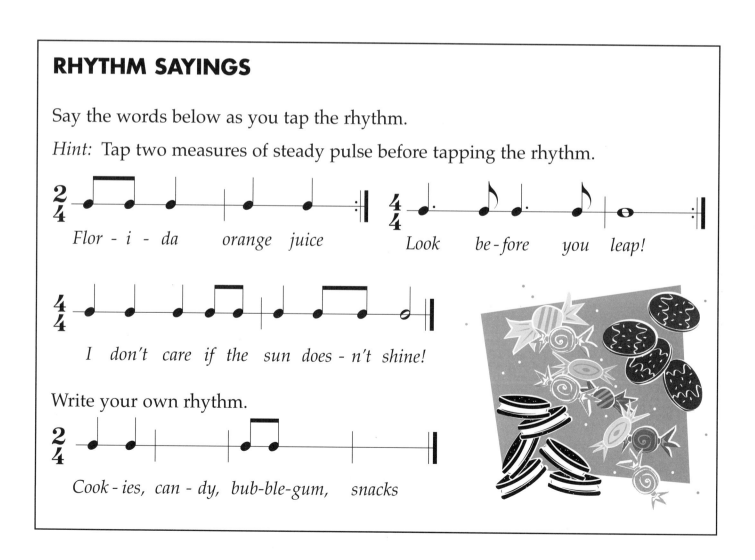

Flor - i - da   orange juice

Look   be - fore   you   leap!

I don't care if the sun does - n't shine!

Write your own rhythm.

Cook - ies, can - dy, bub - ble - gum,   snacks

MORE THAN ONE RHYTHM AT A TIME

Single-line melody

Music with only melody has one rhythm at a time.

Tap:

More than one melody

Music with more than one melody, or music with melody and accompaniment, has more than one rhythm happening at the same time.

Tap:

Melody and accompaniment

Tap:

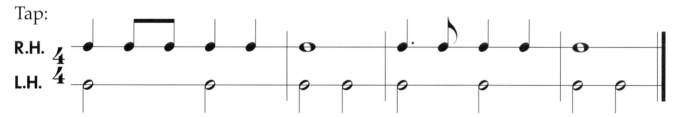

Clues to reading

When tapping rhythms for more than one part at a time, look for spots where the notes line up. That means the notes sound together.

Rests can be a clue to how the rhythms fit together.
Tap this example slowly.

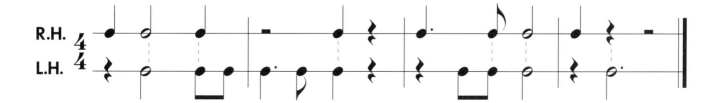

RHYTHM DUOS

Tap and count aloud after completing each part.

Optional: Ask your teacher to tap and speak one part as you tap and speak the other. Then exchange parts and repeat.

1. Jo - seph's   coat   of   ma - ny   col - ored   hues

You write:

Made   him   the   star   of   the   eve - ning   news.

2. News - wor - thy!   News - wor - thy!   News,   news,   news!   Is

You write:

Jo - seph's   coat   of   ma - ny   col - ored   hues!

Rhythm Orchestra (Tapping Duet)

Tap and count each part aloud.

Orchestra rehearsal: If another person is available (your teacher or another student), assign Part 1 to yourself, and Part 2 to the other person. Tap and count aloud together.

More rehearsal: Tap and count this piece with the metronome at a fast tempo.
Write the tempo marking here _____.

CRAZY TUNES

Fix the rhythm of these famous melodies!

London Bridge

correct rhythm _____

Alouette

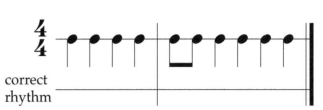

correct rhythm _____

MUSIC CALCULATOR

Add the beats.

○⌣𝅗𝅥 + 𝄽 + 𝅘𝅥𝅭 ♪ = _____ beats

𝅘𝅥 𝅘𝅥𝅮𝅘𝅥𝅮 + 𝅘𝅥𝅮𝅘𝅥𝅮𝅘𝅥𝅮𝅘𝅥𝅮 + 𝅗𝅥𝅭 = _____ beats

▬ + ▬𝅭 + 𝄽𝅭 + 𝄾 = _____ beats

A Saturday Story

Fill in the blanks, then read the story.

*E*arly one Saturday morning, my friend called and woke me at  _____ o'clock.

This was not a very c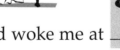_____ t_____ for me to get up! I dressed _____ *presto*,

then waited for my friend to arrive. Patiently I watched the clock strike _____

o'clock, then 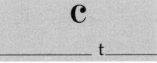 _____. Where was my friend? He certainly was _____ *largo*!

Finally he arrived, but it was too late! I had already gone back to bed.

YOU ARE THE COMPOSER

Say the words below, then write a rhythm that fits.
Then tap and count aloud.

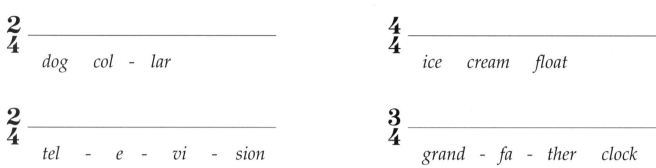

COPYCAT

Imitate the tapping and counting that your teacher does for each example.
Close your eyes and listen carefully.

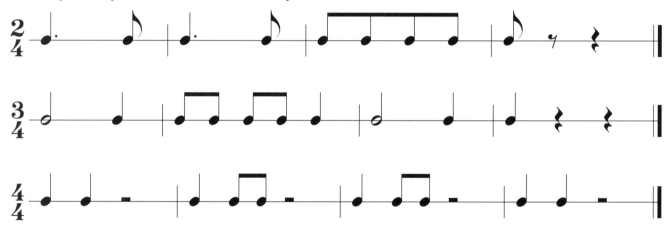

IN THE MOOD

Rhythms can have different tempos (tempi) and dynamics which help create
musical moods. Tap the rhythms below as you follow all the markings.

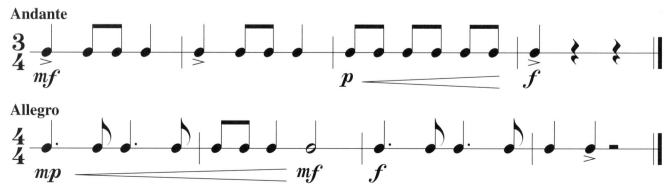

TERMS THAT AFFECT RHYTHM

More Tempo Terms

adagio (ah-DAH-jyoh) - a slow tempo between *lento* and *andante*. (♩ = 62-84)

vivace (vee-VAH-chay) - very quick and lively; faster than *allegro*. (♩ = 130-152)

Terms to Change the Tempo

rit. is the symbol for ***ritardando*** (ree-tahr-DAHN-doh) which means becoming gradually slower.

rall. is the symbol for ***rallentando*** (rahl-len-TAHN-doh) which means the same thing as *ritardando*.

accel. is the symbol for ***accelerando*** (ah-chel-er-AHN-doh) which means becoming gradually faster.

A TEMPO CROSSWORD

All clues are
musical tempos (tempi).

ACROSS

1. Slow tempo (p. 5)
2. Same as *rit.* (p. 33)
6. Lively, quick tempo (p. 21)
7. Very quick, lively tempo (faster than *allegro)* (p. 33)
9. Becoming gradually slower (p. 33)
10. Very fast tempo (p. 5)

DOWN

3. Walking tempo (p. 5)
4. Tempo faster than *largo* (p. 21)
5. Moderate tempo (p. 21)
8. Becoming gradually faster (p. 33)

ANSWERS

Across: 1. largo 2. rall. 6. allegro 7. vivace 9. rit. 10. presto

Down: 3. andante 4. lento 5. moderato 8. accel.

FUN STUDENT CHALLENGES

A test of tempo and rhythm

Points

Score 1 point for each correct answer.

1. Tap and count this rhythm while standing on one leg. _____

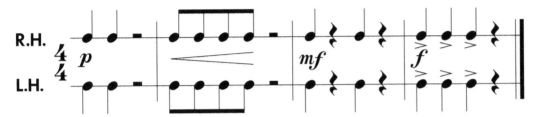

2. Tap the rhythm with both hands, then switch hands. _____

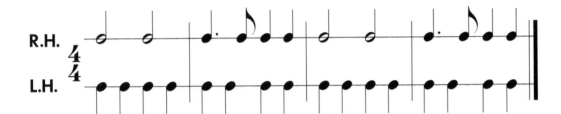

3. Say the words below *presto*, then with a *rall.* _____

   This lit-tle rhy-thm has a nice lit-tle swing. :||

4. Add the beats, then make the beats equal your age (write more beats or take some away). Rewrite the rhythm to equal your age. _____

 = _____ beats

(you write) = _____ *(your age)*

Total Points:

THE MESSY CLOSET ORGANIZER

You have learned many different note values and rests. But somehow they have gotten jumbled up together in a messy closet! It's your job to put them in order, from **shortest** to **longest**. As you "X" each note or rest in the messy closet, "move" it into the neat closet by drawing it.

The Messy Closet

The Neat Closet

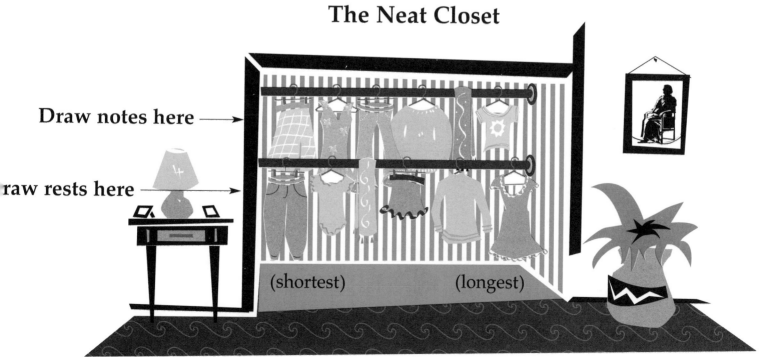

Draw notes here →

raw rests here →

(shortest)   (longest)

Tap Dancers

Tap and count aloud.

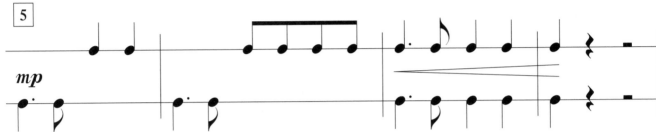

Time to Go Tango!

Tap Dancer's Accompanist

RHYTHM CHECK-UP, BOOK 2

To the teacher:

This rhythm check-up measures how well your student has learned the rhythm concepts in Book 2. If the student has difficulty with any part of the check-up, go back and review that portion of the book before advancing to Book 3.

1. Tap 8 steady beats at an *andante* tempo.

2. Tap and count this rhythm aloud:

3. What is 𝅗𝅥 called, and how many beats does it get in $\frac{4}{4}$ time?

   _____ note   ____ beat(s)

4. What is 𝄾 called, and how many beats does it get in $\frac{4}{4}$ time?

   _____ rest   ____ beat(s)

5. What does the time signature $\frac{3}{4}$ mean?

   3 means _____   4 means _____

6. Where is the strong beat in $\frac{2}{4}$ time?

   _____

7. What is this symbol ♩⌢♩ called, and what does it mean?

   name _____ meaning _____

8. What is 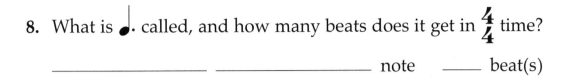 called, and how many beats does it get in $\frac{4}{4}$ time?

_____ _____ note _____ beat(s)

9. Tap and count this rhythm aloud:

10. What is ♩˙ called, and how many beats does it get in $\frac{4}{4}$ time?

_____ _____ rest _____ beat(s)

11. What does $\frac{2}{2}$ mean?

The top 2 means _____. The bottom 2 means _____.

12. Draw another symbol for $\frac{4}{4}$ time.   _____

13. What does *accel.* mean? _____

14. What does *rit.* mean? _____

Report Card

✔ time signatures
✔ rests
✔ tempo terms
✔ counting aloud

FF1236

UNDERWATER WORLD

Write the symbol for
common time on the flag (p. 25).

Write the abbreviation
for *accelerando*
on the octopus (p. 33).

Write the symbol for
cut time on the seahorse (p. 25).

Write the slow tempo
between *lento and andante*
on the snail (p. 33).

Write a *dotted quarter note*
on the treasure chest (p. 18).

Write the tempo for
lively, quick on the fish (p. 21).

Write the abbreviation for *rallentando*
on the turtle's back (p. 33).